Wow, That's Woolly!

SHEEP

Gareth Stevens PUBLISHING

Beth Gottlieb

Please visit our website, www.garethstevens.com. For a free color catalog of all our high-quality books, call toll free 1-800-542-2595 or fax 1-877-542-2596.

Cataloging-in-Publication Data

Names: Gottlieb, Beth.

Title: Sheep / Beth Gottlieb.

Description: New York : Gareth Stevens Publishing, 2023. | Series: Wow, that's woolly! | Includes glossary and index.

Identifiers: ISBN 9781538279519 (pbk.) | ISBN 9781538279533 (library bound) | ISBN 9781538279526 (6pack) | ISBN 9781538279540 (ebook)

Subjects: LCSH: Sheep--Juvenile literature.

Classification: LCC SF375.2 G68 2023 | DDC 636.3--dc23

Published in 2023 by
Gareth Stevens Publishing
29 E. 21st Street
New York, NY 10010

Designer: Olivia Lo Sardo
Editor: Kristen Nelson

Portions of this work were originally authored by Rosaura Esquivel and published as *Merino Sheep*. All new material this edition authored by Beth Gottlieb.

Photo credits: Cover, p. 1 Catchlight Lens/Shutterstock.com; sheep icons ArtHeart/Shutterstock.com; p. 5 Gill Copeland/Shutterstock.com; p. 7 Roman Mikhailiuk/Shutterstock.com; p. 8 Gabor Tinz/Shutterstock.com; p. 9 John Raptosh/Shutterstock.com; p. 10 Jud Goodwin/Shutterstock.com; p. 11 1000 Words/Shutterstock.com; p. 13 PaulLooyen/Shutterstock.com; p. 14 SanyaBuanam/Shutterstock.com; p. 15 WeStudio/Shutterstock.com; p. 17 Dalibor Sevaljevic/Shutterstock.com; p. 18 sureman/Shutterstock.com; p. 19 John Carnemolla/Shutterstock.com; p. 21 nnattalli/Shutterstock.com.

Printed in the United States of America

CPSIA compliance information: Batch #CSGS23: For further information, contact Gareth Stevens, New York, New York, at 1-800-542-2595.

CONTENTS

Words in the glossary appear in **bold** type the first time they are used in the text.

THINK WOOL!

When asked to picture a woolly animal, most people think of sheep first. Sheep are well known for having a puffy, soft coat. Their coats are made of wool. Wool is the fine, soft, wavy or curly hair that forms the coats of sheep and other animals.

Though all sheep have a coat, not all grow wool people are able to use. Some have more hair than wool. There are also some sheep that have very fine wool that is especially prized and **valuable**.

PULL BACK THE WOOL

Depending on the kind of sheep it comes from, wool can be scratchy or soft.

When wool is cut from a sheep, it's called shearing.

SHEEP TYPES

All modern-day sheep come from two wild species, or kinds, of sheep: mouflon and urials. People created different breeds, or types, of sheep through **selective breeding**. Many different kinds of sheep can be found all over the world.

Some sheep are kept for meat. Sheep meat is called mutton, so these breeds are known as mutton-type sheep. Breeds that are kept for their wool are called wool-type sheep. Wool-type breeds are sorted into groups based on the kind of wool they produce.

PULL BACK THE WOOL

All sheep in South America and Australia are **domesticated**.

Wild sheep still live in the mountains of Asia, Europe, Africa, and North America.

DIFFERENT LOOKS

Because there are so many different kinds of sheep, breeds can look very different from one another. In some breeds, both males and females have horns. In others, just males have horns. Other types may not grow horns at all!

Full-grown sheep range greatly in size. They can grow to between 80 and 400 pounds (36 and 181 kg)! Most domestic sheep are white. But sheep can have wool that is black, gray, brown, or red. Some sheep may have light or white wool but a different colored face and legs.

PULL BACK THE WOOL

Jacob sheep have dark spots!

The bighorn sheep grows horns that can weigh 30 pounds (14 kg)!

WHAT TO EAT

Sheep are herbivores, which means they eat only plants. They eat seeds and grass. Sheep are ruminants. They chew their food, swallow it, and then bring it back up to chew and swallow again! They have a stomach with four chambers, or parts. This helps them break down the food they eat.

Sheep often live in groups called herds. They like places that are dry and high up. In Asia, sheep called urials are found at heights of more than 19,000 feet (5,791 m)!

Sheep often **graze** in a group.

FAMILY LIFE

Male sheep are called rams, females are called ewes, and babies are called lambs. Sheep herds may be made up of just ewes and lambs. These may have as many as 100 sheep in them! Male sheep have their own herds. These are called bachelor herds.

Sheep are **mammals**. Ewes usually give birth to one to three lambs at a time. Sheep reach adulthood when they're about a year old. Most sheep live for about 12 years.

PULL BACK THE WOOL

The oldest known sheep lived to be 23!

Lambs are able to walk minutes after birth.

SHEEP AND PEOPLE

Sheep were domesticated by 5000 BCE. In addition to meat, sheep were raised for their milk. Sheep's milk has been used to drink as well as make many kinds of cheese.

For thousands of years, people have raised sheep for wool. People shear this wool and make it into cloth. Since ancient times, wool has been prized for its warmth and **durability**. During the **Middle Ages**, the wool trade was a major industry in Europe.

Sheep are still raised today for meat, milk, and wool—just like in ancient times!

SHEARING SHEEP

Today, domesticated sheep are sheared each year in the spring. Shearing allows people to use a sheep's wool. It also helps keep sheep clean and able to keep their body temperature steady.

After the wool is cut from the sheep, it's cleaned. Next, the fleece is carded. Carding straightens the tangled pieces of wool and lengthens them. Spinning is the process by which wool is made into yarn. Large-scale spinning is done on machines. However, many people spin wool at home.

PULL BACK THE WOOL

Lanolin, a natural grease, is removed from wool when it's cleaned. Lanolin is used to make makeup!

The wool sheared from one sheep is called a fleece.

MERINO WOOL

Wool is measured in small units called microns. The smaller the **diameter** of a wool **fiber**, the finer and softer the wool.

Merino wool is some of the softest and finest wool in the world. A single Merino hair is three times finer than the average human hair! Merino wool is soft, light, and breathable, which means air can flow through it. It's sought after because it can keep the wearer warm during cold seasons and cool in hot ones.

PULL BACK THE WOOL

The Rambouillet is a fine wool sheep that's common in the United States.

Today, Australia is the leading producer of Merino wool. Australian Merino wool is the highest-quality sheep's wool in the world.

WOOL USES

Once wool is made into yarn, it can be used to make clothing like sweaters, hats, and socks. The finer the wool, the softer these items will be. Wool fibers that have a thicker diameter can still be used to make clothing, but they may feel scratchier! Coarser, or rougher, wool can also be used to make rugs or **insulation**.

Sheep's wool is very useful. It's also a **material** that does not harm Earth. Sheep's wool can be reused, and it's **biodegradable**. What a wonderful wool!

PULL BACK THE WOOL

Wool doesn't catch fire, making it very safe for use in houses.

Sheep's wool continues to be an important material for making goods and clothing.

GLOSSARY

biodegradable: Able to be slowly broken down into very small parts by natural processes.

diameter: The distance from one side of a round object to another through its center.

domesticated: Bred and raised for use by people.

durability: The ability to last a long time.

fiber: A thin thread of natural or human-made material that can be used to make cloth.

graze: To eat grass or other plants growing in a field.

insulation: A material that surrounds something to stop heat, electricity, or sound from passing through.

mammal: A warm-blooded animal that has a backbone and hair, breathes air, and feeds milk to its young.

material: Matter from which something is made.

Middle Ages: A time in European history from about 500 to 1500.

selective breeding: Bringing together male and female animals with wanted features so that they'll have babies with those features.

valuable: Worth money.

FOR MORE INFORMATION

Books

Greenwood, Nancy. *Prizewinning Sheep.* New York, NY: PowerKids Press, 2023.

Toolen, Avery. *From Sheep to Sock.* Minneapolis, MN: Bullfrog Books, 2022.

Websites

How Woolly Sweaters Are Made

thekidshouldseethis.com/post/how-woolly-sweaters-are-made-the-magic-of-making

Watch a video about how sweaters get made from sheep's wool.

Sheep Facts for Kids

www.dkfindout.com/us/animals-and-nature/domesticated-animals/sheep/

Read more about sheep and other domesticated animals.

INDEX